Youth Ministry is Easy! and nine other lies is both practical and inspiring! Aaron Shaver writes with the wisdom of personal experience and the passion of divine calling. I hope this book finds its place in the hands of many a youth pastor and all those who love youth!

Pastor Jim Thomas
The Village Chapel
Nashville, TN

Aaron Shaver has brought together the wisdom of years of youth ministry, experienced for several different perspectives, and condensed it into this highly readable book. This is a sure footed guide. There is not a single misstep in his observations. Everything is solid and essential. Anyone interested in ministering to youth will find this an invaluable resource.

Pastor Ronnie Meek
Springhouse Worship and Arts Center
Smyrna, TN

YOUTH MINISTRY IS EASY!
AND NINE OTHER LIES

Aaron Shaver

YOUTH MINISTRY IS EASY!

AND NINE OTHER LIES

WordCrafts

Youth Ministry Is Easy!
                and nine other lies
Copyright © 2013
Aaron Shaver

Cover art by Ted Woods
Design & photography by David Warren

All rights reserved. No part of this book may be reproduced, stored in a retrieval system, or transmitted in any form or by any means – electronic, mechanical, photocopy, recording, or otherwise – without the prior written permission of the publisher. The only exception is brief quotations for review purposes.

Published by WordCrafts Press
Tullahoma, TN 37388
www.wordcrafts.net

CONTENTS

Introduction	1
1. Youth Ministry Is Easy!	4
2. Parents Are Your Worst Enemy	15
3. You Can't Expect Much from Teens	28
4. Great Youth Pastors Go Solo	37
5. Teens Hate Learning About the Bible	47
6. Losing Cool Points with the Teens is Fatal	55
7. Your Personal Spiritual Health Can Wait	62
8. Bigger, Faster and Louder Equals Better	71
9. Youth Ministry is Just a Stepping Stone to a *Real* Pastor's Job	78
10. Youth Ministry is a Failed Experiment	86
Thanks	94

To Elaina, my wife, who discovered that ministry would always be a part of our journey from the first day she met me. And, she still said, "Yes."

INTRODUCTION

So here is how this book works. Each chapter heading is a common misconception about youth ministry.

Or to be perfectly frank, a lie.

I hope to debunk those lies and give you some tips that might help you to be a better minister, parent, youth worker or church member who wonders, *What's up with the kids these days?*

During my years serving as a youth minister in a variety of different churches - from small to large, fundamental to more, shall we say, expressive, - one thing has remained constant: there are plenty of misconceptions, myths, half-truths, un-truths and outright lies about what a youth pastor is, and what he or she is supposed to do.

Most of these attitudes, misconceptions and... - alright, let's just say it, lies - are not the result of some evil conspiracy. Nor are they the intentional manipulations of a single person. Instead, they are the natural outgrowth of preconceived notions, false assumptions and romanticized expectations of people who are already in professional ministry.

And would-be youth pastors.
And church members.
And parents.
And teens.

Over the years these preconceived notions, false assumptions and romanticized expectations have taken on the weight of gravitas of age until they are accepted as Gospel. We have become so accustomed to the drone of the oft-repeated that we don't realize we are all repeating the same lies about this relatively new institution we call Youth Ministry.[1]

This book is an attempt to clear the air and provide you - the youth pastor, adult volunteer, parent or anyone who desires to work in youth ministry - with an honest look at what you are getting yourself into.

In this book, you will read anecdotes from my own personal experiences in youth ministry. But I'm not narcissistic enough to believe my experiences are the be-all-and-end-all of youth ministry. I also draw on the plethora of experience from a host of other youth pastors who were gracious enough to share some of the lessons they learned in the trenches.

Before we get started, this is probably a good place to tell you what this book is not. It's not a doctrinal thesis. You won't find me musing over the

---

[1] If you consider just the history of the Church in America, let alone the rest of the world, youth ministry as we know it is a very new phenomenon. Youth ministries didn't start operating as a specialized ministry of the Church until the 1970s. That's only around 40 years from the time this book was written.

finer points of God's sovereignty versus man's free will or pondering the merits of topical preaching versus exegetical preaching. Those are great discussions, to be sure, but there are plenty of fine books on those subjects written by people who are far better qualified to speak to those issues.

What you will find are practical and applicable lessons for your ministry.

You'll discover tried-and-true tools and techniques that have already been used in the field by successful youth pastors. Maybe even better - we'll tell you what *didn't* work for us.

Sure, you could learn it the hard way. There are still plenty of ditches out there for you to fall in. But the truth is, we'll already stepped in those holes, and we're happy to tell you where they are, so you can avoid them. Let's face it, experience is a great teacher but failure is the most memorable.

> *"Experience is the teacher of all things."*
> *– Julius Caesar*

As you read this book, I think you'll find your call to work with teens is much more challenging - and much more rewarding - than you anticipated.

Let's get started, shall we?

LIE #1

YOUTH MINISTRY IS EASY!

You may have been shocked by the title of the book when you first picked it up. I certainly hope so. That was my intent.

Shock is a perfectly understandable reaction to such an assertion, but the truth is, youth ministry is not easy. Youth ministry is hard work.

"Why would a youth minister tell other youth workers and potential youth workers that doing youth ministry is hard," you might wonder. "That doesn't sound very encouraging."

Well, yes and no.

No one, particularly those of us in the ministry, should hide from the truth. And the truth is, no one is encouraged by a lie. It's far more encouraging to know what you are getting into from the get-go, than to get knee-deep in the hoopla before you find out youth work is messy.

By telling you what to expect, I hope to empower you to face the challenges ahead. Anyone who tells you that youth ministry is easy is just preparing the lamb for the slaughter. Telling you that youth ministry is hard might sound harsh, but as the old

Saturday morning cartoon hero used to tell you, "Now you know...and knowing is half the battle."

Consider this: On average, youth pastors in paid staff positions at a church only stick around for 4 years.

Four years.

Let that sink in for a minute.[2]

Now think about how that plays out in reality. How many churches invested how much time and money - and how many youth groups invested their trust and emotional energy - in a youth pastor, only to have that youth pastor leave after what amounts to one high school generation?

Kind of makes you stop and ask, why?

Maybe it's because aspiring youth ministers have bought into the lie that youth ministry is all fun and games; that it's easy.

Nobody wants to see members of their church's ministry team become burned-out, frustrated and ineffective. Nobody wants to see their youth pastor become just another statistic.

And if you are a youth pastor, you want to protect yourself from that same kind of burn-out and prevent your church from experiencing staff turn-over.

I've made a concentrated effort to meet and pick the brains of several accomplished pastors in various

---

[2] According to Josh Griffin, High School Pastor at Saddleback Church. Check out more of what his has to say on this fact at http://www.morethandodgeball.com/tag/average-stay-of-a-youth-pastor/

areas of ministry. There's nothing like swapping stories over a meal with spiritual giants who have walked this path for years for gaining ministry insight and practical wisdom.

I sat down at lunch with Pat Rowland. Pat is the Family Ministries Pastor at Woodside Bible Church in Troy, Michigan. Pat knows a thing or two about developing God's people; about teaching and mentoring the next generation of Christ's followers.

"Being a youth pastor is so incredibly difficult," he confided. "The person who takes that job is almost always the youngest and least experienced person on staff at a church. Their job description requires that they appeal to two fundamentally different audiences: they have to be cool and fun for the teens, but they also have to earn the respect of the parents. The youth pastor has to be a visionary, a great communicator, theologically solid, a discerning teacher, a mentor, a disciplinarian and a number cruncher - all while ministering to the most volatile age group in the church. Nobody is made to do all of that."[3]

Youth ministry is *not* easy. But I don't blame you if you were misinformed.

If you grew up in a youth group during your teenage years, as I did, you probably have a skewed view of the youth pastor's job. Most of us think of youth ministry as pizza parties, lock-ins, camp

---

[3] Pat Rowland ministers to multiple generations by intentionally investing in families. You can read more about how he does that here, http://patrowland.me/

retreats and refereeing the occasional dating drama.

Why? Because, that's all we remember from our teenage years in youth group. But what we saw from the outside had very little to do with what happened on the inside.

The truth is; you don't go into youth ministry because it is fun. You go into youth ministry because you are called to it. You have a calling to minister to both teens *and* their families. You're called to be a mentor, a teacher *and* a shepherd. You're called to invest your mind, heart, body and time into the lives of the next generation.

Youth ministry is a high calling that requires a high investment. As Luke 14:28 admonishes, a wise man counts the cost before starting a building project. If you feel called into youth ministry, it's a good idea to find out what it will cost you before you dip your toes in those waters.

Jasper Rains of Get Real Youth Ministries at Parkway Baptist Church has more than 18 years in the trenches of youth ministry. He puts it this way:

"So, as I ask myself what youth ministry is really about, I see faces and lives that have been touched and changed over my 18 years of service. It is the faces of lives changed and the shadows of the lives still to come that encourage me to continue on in light of difficult times.

"You see, youth ministry is also really about me. It is about God working in my life. It is about God changing me and using me to advance the Kingdom.

He uses me in spite of my inadequacies. He uses me in spite of my sin. He uses me even though I am not worthy at all. He uses me because youth ministry is really about being obedient to His call."[4]

I believe the ideas set out in this book are critical to your success as a youth worker - rather than simply as a resource to help you get the job done, but to also help you keep yourself emotionally and spiritually healthy.

Youth pastors and youth workers experience a high rate of burn-out. While most of us would like to think that it's due to outside pressures and high expectations placed on us by parents and other members of the church staff, the truth is it's mostly self-inflicted.

Most youth pastors I've talked to, when looking back on their first years of youth ministry, agree that they worked longer hours, asked for less help and made a whole lot more mistakes than was necessary. There are a lot of reasons for this, but few excuses. It's usually caused by the dangerous combination of inexperience and the need to prove yourself to others.

I know I was guilty of this.

---

[4] Jasper Rains is a youth pastor in the St. Louis area. You really should check out more his thoughts and musings on youth ministry at his blog: *Jasper Speaks*
http://youthministerman.blogspot.com/

To be honest with you, my greatest concern during my first year of youth ministry was that people thought I wasn't working hard enough. It's sad to think about all those late hours stressing over every little detail; second-guessing every decision; being too afraid to ask for help.

Even sadder; it was all in my head.

Allow this book to give you permission to relax, trust and reach out to parents, mentors and other members of the church staff for help. This can be a challenge. After all, one of the biggest problems when you start out in youth ministry is that you don't know what you don't know.

Like a lot of youth pastors, when I started out I was told to "just run with it... and ask for help if you really need it."

The first church where I acted as youth pastor didn't mentor me. There was no one there to show me the ropes; no one to explain the best way to plan and grow a youth ministry. There was no one there to tell me how to avoid mistakes, but boy, there were plenty of people there to let me know when I made one.

Unfortunately, a lot of churches don't train their staff. People don't naturally offer up the information needed for others to succeed. It's not so much that they don't want you to succeed, as it is they have their own issues to deal with. You've gotta dig for information. So, dear youth pastor, don't be afraid to ask questions. Don't be afraid to dig.

Object Lesson:
What You Don't Know Can Get You Killed

A few years ago, I was helping a friend baby-sit his nephews. The youngest, a 7-year old named Cody, asked me to play video games with him. He had a game already picked out - a first-person-shooter with an ominous sounding name like Desert Warfare Apocalypse...or something similar.

I was afraid to admit to the little guy that I wasn't much of a gamer. In fact, I hadn't played video games since I was his age. Video games just never held my interest, even as a child, and since gaming has come a long way since Super NES I figured I'd be totally lost trying to keep up with this 7-year old in some hyper-realistic covert desert sniper operation.

I was right.

Cody, grabbed a seat on the carpet in front of the TV, loaded the game and there was no turning back.

We were dropped into the middle of the action. Our mission, should we choose to accept it, was to sneak up on an enemy bunker and take out their heavy artillery gun - hopefully without being detected and killed in the process.

This was intense stuff! The slightest misstep or a head raised at the wrong time would give away our position and bring down a hail of enemy gunfire that would quickly and violently end our tediously realistic mission.

Cody's nostrils flared and his fingers flickered over the game controls with a feverish intensity that kinda scared me a little, if the truth be told. I, on the other hand, was dead weight. I didn't contribute to the success of our mission at all, and Cody had no qualms about letting me know it.

Every few seconds I had to ask a question.

So, Cody, which button do I push to make him duck?

Which button shoots my weapon?

Why can't I see where he's going?

After several frustrated responses from Cody, I realized he was in no mood to teach this *noob* how to play the game. This 7-year-old had no time to stop and teach me. He just wanted to play.

After almost 15 intense, and tedious, minutes of low-crawling, reconnoitering and stealthily slipping between burnt-out obstacles of the video-enhanced hyper-reality of an urban desert war zone - without firing a shot or getting any help from Cody -I'd had enough. I took it upon myself to do the unexpected, to take initiative, to launch a surprise attack and take the enemy unawares!

And, yeah, I'll admit, I was a little bored and it was a little mean.

While we were still creeping up on the enemy, I used what little first-person-shooter game-play skill I had acquired and made my avatar jump up, run frantically into the kill zone, firing his weapon with wild abandon.

"What are you doing?!" Cody shouted, panicked that all his plans were in ruins.

"Suicide run," I yelled back. "Come on! Follow

me, boys! Over the top! Take 'em all down! Remember the Alamo!"

"Stop it," he pleaded. "You'll get us killed!"

"Killed?" I scoffed. "It's a video game. Let's have some fun. Just start shooting!"

At this point Cody had no choice but to break cover and return fire at an enemy we couldn't see. I ran head-long into 'em, firing at will.

"Aaron, what are you doing?" Cody whined as the hail of digital gunfire peppered down on us, depleting our soldiers' life-meters.

More gunfire, rockets, explosions, pixilated chaos and dismembered body parts filled the screen as our respective soldiers met their doom in Desert Warfare Apocalypse. Cody slammed his game controller on the floor and stormed out of the room.

"Well, that was fun," I said. "Wanna play again?"

If you are new to youth ministry, or any kind of ministry, my experience with Cody might not be all that unfamiliar to you. Chances are you don't know how things work. Even if you are a seasoned youth minister, if you are embarking on a new ministry at a different church, you probably don't know how things work in that new environment.

In most cases there are *Codys* in place who already know how things work - pastors, administrators, people in other leadership positions and parents. But they might not think to share that information with you. They might be too busy with their own obligations, or they might just assume you already know how things get done.

You need the people in leadership/pastors to explain to you 'what's what' in the ministry world where you are serving. Don't be afraid to ask them the questions that will help you succeed in your mission before a hail of spiritual gunfire rains fire down upon your head.

What questions?

Glad you asked. That was the first one.

This book is designed to help you formulate the right questions, and to help you respond with the answers so you can address such things as:

How to keep the teens interested while earning the respect of their parents.

How to approach teaching tough topics in the Bible.

How to recruit a team of volunteers and, after they are recruited, what to do with them.

As you work your way through this book, let me be perfectly clear about one thing: This book is *not* the definitive word on youth ministry.

I'm neither naïve enough or arrogant enough to assume that I know how you should minister to the young people God has placed in your charge. That's a journey God has tailored to you, the young people He has placed in your care and the families of those teens.

But I do believe this book can help you more clearly assess where you are as you begin your career in youth ministry; and if you will let it, it can offer you a true and illusion-free base to help launch you into the most rewarding journey you can imagine.

LIE #2
PARENTS ARE YOUR WORST ENEMY

There are two secrets every youth worker should know:

1 - Youth ministry is not simply a ministry to the youth. It's a ministry to parents too.
2 - Parents want to be on your side.

Over the past few years, I've heard a lot of variations on the title given to the person in charge of ministering to young people:
Youth Pastor
Youth Director
Student Pastor.
All of these might be appropriate for the position, but the one I like most is:
Pastor to Families with Students.
Yes, it is mouthful, but as titles go, it's the most accurate one for the job description.
Youth ministry is not just a ministry to teens at a church. At its most effective, it's a ministry to the families of the teens. That includes parents and siblings who might be older or younger.

You don't honestly believe you're equipped or called to minister to the most volatile age group in the church without also ministering to the family they go home to everyday, do you? After all, if God thought it was important to "turn the hearts of the fathers to their children, and the hearts of the children to their fathers,"[5] then it's important for us to do the same.

I can understand if you think focusing your time and attention on ministering to grown adults doesn't sound much like youth ministry. The very term, *youth ministry*, conjures up visions of over-night lock-ins, pizzas and coke, dating drama, cheesy get-to-know-you-games. Youth ministry is, after all, *youth* ministry, right?

Well, yes.

And no.

You can't effectively minister to the kids and forget the folks who bring those kids to church. Most of the time the parents were the very people who introduced them to Christianity in the first place. If you're going to minister to young people, you have to do so along with their parents.

Object Lesson:
Prepare The Soil Before You Plant The Wheat.

Growing up in Smyrna, Tennessee in the 1990s, I witnessed my own youth group, under the direction of youth pastor Pat Hood, experience phenomenal

---

[5] Malachi 4: 5-6

and rapid growth.[6] It exploded from 60 kids to 260 in just two years.

You don't experience that kind of growth without some growing pains, and a lot of changes.

Changes in the size of the programming.

Changes that stretched the youth ministry budget.

Changes that forced our discipleship ministry to adapt to the influx of new teens.

Can you guess what remained constant throughout all of this growth? That's right - the parents. Before our church experienced the sudden addition of hundreds of teens to our youth ministry, Pat Hood already had parents attending our Wednesday night youth services by the dozen. Pat knew the value of having a strong parental presence in the youth group events.

I remember walking into the old fellowship hall where the teens met for youth group every week. For every 10 teens there was at least one adult in the room.

When your parents have a presence in your youth ministry, it adds immense value to your efforts. One of the most obvious benefits is crowd control. Face it, one youth worker versus 30 or more teens is dangerous - for you and for the kids.

---

[6] Check out what Pat is doing these days at Life Point Church in Smyrna, TN by going to his blog http://pathood.org/

Another benefit is, when parents are present in your events and activities, they're more likely to stay informed about the youth ministry schedule and vision. Their added involvement may even help identify trouble spots and emerging issues before you see them.

Perhaps even more important, the presence of parents at your ministry events subliminally tells teens that what happens in youth ministry is safe *and* important. It says the parents care about what goes on in their children's lives. There's no substitute for the actual presence of parents in your ministry.

Of course, not all parents are invested or even interested in their kids' lives. As sad as that sounds, you will find it to be the truth for some kids in your ministry. But lack of engagement in the church or in their teenager's life doesn't excuse you from reaching out to them. We'll talk more about un-engaged parents later. For now, just assume that most of the parents of teens in your church want to be your #1 fans!

Parents need to feel that you are trustworthy. Parents want to know that you care about the physical and emotional well-being of their child just as much as they do.

Notice that I used the word *child* instead of *teenager* or *student*. It was intentional. Parents typically still see their teen as a child; one with a curfew and a weird sense of fashion, but a child nonetheless. Even if the teen, you and the rest of society may not technically consider these teens as children, their parents still do. And the parents' opinion trumps society's opinion every time.

To help you get inside the minds and hearts of parents, I'd like you to hear from one. Ronei Harden is a wonderful wife and mother who personally saw me grow as a youth pastor during my time at Springhouse Worship and Arts Center in Smyrna, Tennessee. She's written an open letter to youth pastors. Whether you're in youth ministry full-time, part-time or serve as a volunteer, you can benefit from reading her words:

It is an awesome thing to see a young person's life transformed by the Word of God. Being a part of that process is an honor and a privilege. Few people realize the commitment and dedication it takes to raise a child, especially in today's world. Likewise, the role of a youth pastor requires the same, if not more, commitment and dedication to the cause. Both roles are under daily assault on all fronts; spiritual, social and internal.

I am a mother of two; ages twenty-four and seventeen, and have over ten years experience working with children of all ages as a private tutor. I've also had the privilege of working alongside many great leaders in both the corporate world and in ministry. During those years, I've learned some vital tips that have helped me develop my own business serving families. I'd like to share them with you.

You are not the parent - *When you have a true calling on your life, and that calling involves children,* it's easy to let your heart get caught up in the moment. Whether you are a hired teacher or a youth pastor, you are providing service to the parent and the child. Open communication with the parents is vital. Legally, the children belong to the parents, whether they are distant and uninvolved or committed and consuming. This important boundary lifts a huge burden off of the tutor/youth pastor's shoulders. God has not called you to be the parent, but to come alongside the parents and walk with them for a season of time. It allows you to help the parents in their endeavors. You'll find that your job will also mean ministering to the parents as well as the students.

If you haven't experienced it, you can't teach it - It sounds cliché, but it's true. I personally always found it ironic that a twenty-something year old single youth pastor was trying to tell me, a 40-year old married mother of two, how I should raise my kids. I always smiled and thanked them for their heartfelt zeal, but I think I marveled more at the fact that they were blissfully ignorant. Think of your job as being called, not to instruct the parents but, to empower them.

Your example speaks louder than your words - Again, sounds cliché, but this is true in any occupation. Be genuine. I purposely let my students see me in situations where I don't have all the answers. What I try to let my students see is the process of how I seek out answers to questions, or solutions to problems. I also invite them to help me, to join my team and seek the answers together. Live an example of integrity.

Live a life you want your students to emulate. There's nothing more detrimental to a student-teacher/pastor relationship than for them to see hypocrisy. You can't sleep with your boyfriend/girlfriend and then try to lead a small group. Teenagers have amazing discernment and can spot someone who is fake or phony. They also have high regard for people who are real, trustworthy and dependable.

You aren't their buddy; you're their leader *- Once again, it comes down to realizing the divine limits that have been set in the role of tutor/youth pastor. It's easy to feel young again when you are in a room of kids or teens. Jesus reminded his disciples of this when he said, "Let the little children come to me." It's that child-like quality, that sweet spirit in the heart of the child that Jesus loved most. It is our job as tutors and pastors to educate, encourage and protect that from the enemy. Sometimes that means making those difficult decisions that bring correction in a student's life. When your role as tutor/youth pastor is clearly defined, students can receive correction from you with the proper attitude.*

Ronei's words carry great weight. Invested parents like Ronei are a blessing to your ministry. To put it in business terms, parents are your real customers...not the teens. If you want to make a sale, you've got to know what your customer wants. Learn what your customer, the parent, wants. What they want should be what you want....and what the teens need.

As youth workers, we might approach ministry with the intent to earn coolness points with the teens while laying down some spiritual truths that'll wow them. Parents come from a different place entirely. Parents do not feel the need to impress their child with any coolness factor.

At least, they should not.

A parent's first priority regarding their teen is safety.

A parent's first concern for their kids is usually safety.

Not spiritual maturity.

Not Biblical knowledge.

Not church activity or youth group involvement.

You may or may not be a parent yourself. If you are not, then the burden is really on you to earn the parent's trust. Parents, like most of us, value personal experience. And if you don't have the personal experience of being a parent, well, they might have a hard time trusting you with their child.

If you are a parent, you have an added advantage because the other parents will assume you share their concern for a child's well-being. That's a great thing, but don't abuse this advantage. In fact, let me encourage you to make every effort to prove yourself worthy of their confidence.

For example, let's view a seemingly innocuous

communication from a concerned parent's perspective. Let's say a father of one of your teens calls your phone and leaves a voicemail saying he wants to talk about the upcoming mission trip. You don't call him back that day because you're just too busy but promise yourself you'll return his call first thing tomorrow. The next day passes, then the next. Three days later, you still haven't returned his call. You meant too, but things just came up, ya know?

But, why worry? Tomorrow is Sunday and you'll see him at church in the morning and discuss it with him then. Unfortunately, you missed him at church. You finally call on Monday evening to discuss the upcoming mission trip.

But right now, dad is thinking, *If it takes a week for you to return my call now, what will it be like if I have to call you while you're on the mission trip with my precious little girl in another country?*

You might have heard the old saying, *Don't sweat the small stuff; and it's all small stuff.*

Don't kid yourself. It might all be *small stuff*, but how you handle the *small stuff* now, communicates how you'll handle the *big stuff* later, when it really counts.

Do you really think parents don't notice the little things?

Trust me. They do!

While parents can be your biggest critics, that is

only because they *want* to be your biggest supporters.

Do you remember as a child when your parents would discipline you, then say something like, *I'm doing this only because I love you?*

It is possible for parents to be critical of what you are doing, what you are saying or how you are behaving because they love their children...and because they love your ministry. If you're doing something involving their children that they don't like, expect to hear about it from the parents.

And that's a good thing. Seriously!

I realized this only by experience when a mother stopped me in the church hall with a complaint about the style of music we used during our Wednesday night teen services. We obviously didn't see eye-to-eye on the subject. I quickly realized that we were at an impasse and would likely leave this conversation in disagreement. But in the middle of that confrontation, when I was almost ready to tune her out, I realized how very valuable her opinion was to me.

We didn't agree, this mother and I, and we didn't have to. Honestly, I don't think she entirely expected me to simply comply with her wishes. But she certainly *did* expect me to at least listen to her concerns.

I was smacked in the face by the realization that I truly did *not* know what was best for her child. Her teen didn't live under my roof. I did not carry the responsibility of raising that child. That mother did.

She knew what was best for her child – not me. And even if she didn't know what was best, she probably knew better than I did.

The *problem* this mother brought to me really was a blessed opportunity for me to receive some honest feed-back on the ministry program we had in place for the teens.

Think of it this way:

1) This parent cared enough about her child to face me with this issue, and;

2) This parent cared enough about me and how I led the teen ministry to confront me about this issue.

I might have remained blissfully ignorant if the parent had chosen to remain silent. What a loss that would have been for the teen and for me.

Real life shows us plenty of examples of parents who don't care about the spiritual maturity or safety of their children. Unfortunately, you will encounter a fair share of teens in your youth ministry whose parents are noticeably absent from the church scene.

Not every parent is excited to receive a phone call or email from you. Some parents are convinced that the youth ministry events at your church are nothing more than a glorified baby-sitting service for teenagers.

Remember two things:

1) *You must engage these parents.* The teenagers' overall experience in your youth ministry needs parental involvement.

2) *You won't win 'em all.* It is the job of the Holy Spirit to change hearts. Don't count it as failure if

your attempts to contact/communicate/engage with parents is met with less than stellar results.

Listen to parents, because they know their kids better than you do. *Include* parents in your ministry because they want to feel welcomed and be informed. *Minister* to parents because they need it.

That's right. You are responsible for reaching out to them with words of guidance and encouragement. When you reach out to the parents it frees them up to support your ministry and get behind you as you move forward. And you will need that support in the coming days. You really will.

Now, having said so much about getting parents involved in your youth ministry, let me make the following caveat perfectly clear: Not every parent should be directly involved with the teens in your ministry. You will experience circumstances where a parent (or other adult) may need to be asked to withdraw from involvement with the youth ministry.

A parent, just like a child, may have a behavioral problem which, while not necessarily a direct threat to their own child, may be distracting or even hurtful to other teens. You might experience something as serious as a parent who exhibits threatening behavior to the teens or other adults. Some parents who faithfully volunteer can become overloaded with just life-stuff. This can trigger burn-out. It happens.

The types of situations that may warrant

removing a parent (temporarily or permanently) from involvement in youth ministry are so varied that I wouldn't even dare to attempt to give you a singular and encompassing way to address it.

But I will say the gravity of this issue is such that it needs to be taken to your church's pastoral staff and fervently prayed over.

These are the types of situations that go beyond one person's decision-making power. Take the issue to someone with a greater level of spiritual authority, such as your pastor or immediate supervisor. Let them determine whether your particular situation is really a question of a parent's prerogative on how to raise their child, or whether the safety and integrity of the youth ministry is being compromised.

LIE #3
YOU CAN'T EXPECT MUCH FROM TEENS

Every generation seems to look down on the subsequent up-and-coming generation. This is nothing new. But, why do we do it? Do we really think that the younger generation is lazier than we were at their age? Or do we think they are any less intelligent or less capable than previous generation?

It's true that norms change, styles change and behaviors change. But, let's face it - immature teens have always been, and always will be, immature teens.

The children now love luxury; they have bad manners, contempt for authority; they show disrespect for elders and love chatter in place of exercise. Children are now tyrants, not the servants of their households. They no longer rise when elders enter the room. They contradict their parents, chatter before company, gobble up dainties at the table, cross their legs, and tyrannize their teachers. - Socrates, c. 400 BC

As a youth worker, you are going to be overexposed to the immaturity and *it's all about me* attitudes that are inherit with this age group. Don't let this exposure to their narcissism cause you to lower the bar for them, or even worse, write them off entirely.

It is easy to grow numb to your calling of minister to teens and forego challenging them toward a closer and better life with Christ. But, for the sake of these teens, you can't do that. Do not buy into the lie that you should not, or can not, expect more from them.

Historically speaking, teens these days read more than any other generation before them, although it might be true that what they are reading is more like sleaze than literature. They are also busier than previous generations.

The average high schooler spends 35 to 40 hours per week in school, and invests another 8 to 10 hours studying or doing homework. That doesn't count the time required for dance rehearsals, ball practice, social networking, civic volunteerism, video games, a part-time job and some hang out time with their friends.

Needless to say, they have the capacity to busy their lives with *more*. More reading, more responsibilities, more sleaze, more gossip, more noise, more, more, more! So, why can't we, as youth ministers, expect more spiritual growth from them?

Maybe we're just unsure how to channel this busy energy in teens toward active engagement in the Gospel message. But, even worse, I think some youth workers lower the bar for their teens because it gives themselves an out when their teens don't grow spiritually as much as we expect them to.

Bad idea. We can't afford to be blinded by our own disappointment.

In one of my first assignments as a youth pastor, my intern and I had invited a guest speaker on the annual youth ski trip. The speaker was a family man who loved volunteering with youth groups from nearby churches and was known to be a great communicator to teens. While we were on the ski trip I pulled him and my intern aside and confessed to him that our youth group was having trouble.

"Our teens just aren't...engaged. They don't seem to care," I said. "They show up. But, mission trips, worship services...it's like they just check out emotionally and spiritually."

His response caught me off guard.

"Aaron, have you given them a sense of ownership in this ministry?" he asked.

Immediately, I was defensive.

"Well, no," I confessed.

Why would I want a bunch of teenagers to feel like they owned anything? If anything shouldn't I, the youth pastor, possess a sense of ownership in the youth ministry?

He went on to tell me that no one truly *owns* a ministry...but that students in a youth ministry should feel a sense of responsibility for

> *"Every excuse I ever heard made perfect sense to the person who made it."*
> — *Dr. Daniel T. Drubin*

what goes on in their group; a sense of responsibility that is usually only felt when there is a bestowal of ownership.

"When it comes to your youth group, these teens need to feel like, *If I don't do it, it won't get don't. If I don't say it, no one else will.*"

I realized he was right. I knew the teens trusted in me, but they also deferred every bit of responsibility to me. They unplugged because, deep inside, my leadership had made them little more than an audience that needed only to show up to get their weekly fill of *church*.

If you want teens in your youth ministry to meet your expectations of spiritual growth, you must give them a sense of responsibility and ownership for the success or failure of the ministry. Communicate that they are the hands and feet of the ministry. Help them understand that you are only one person, but they are an army of ministers with a responsibility to take ownership of their high calling to serve their church, their school, their peers and the world.

Set the bar high for your teens and communicate those standards. Equip them and encourage them to grow toward those expectations. Outside of their own parents, you should be their biggest source of encouragement.

For the teens whose parents really aren't a source of encouragement, you definitely need to be their biggest champion.

Youth culture in this country, and quite frankly in every other culture and in every other century, has been historically described as rebellious, lazy and apathetic. Young people in America have heard this message for generations.

It was no different for me when I was a teen. And, it was no different for my parents in their day. After a while, we all start to believe this message - so much so that once we grow out of our teen years we turn around and shackle the next generation of teenagers with the same message - regardless of who they truly are or anything they have really done.

Every generation is distinct. Capitalize on that distinction.

This would be a great time for you to break the cycle in your youth group. Every generation of teens - every individual teen, for that matter - is distinct. Capitalize on that distinction.

Look at the teens in your youth ministry. Take an honest assessment of who they are, what activities they like, how they think, what they hope for, what they fear. You'll find in some ways they are no different from any other generation of teenagers that has gone on before them. But in other ways each generation has some unique distinctions.

For instance, the so-called Millennial Generation and the subsequent generation to come behind them tend to be tech savvy and social cause-oriented.

Think about it. How many of your teens have a Facebook account, their own YouTube channel, tweet incessantly and can operate a DSLR camera?

Probably more than you think.

Come to think of it, do you even know what a DSLR camera is? Savvy Savannah, the 14-year old in your youth group does.

A bright youth worker would set the bar high for this teen. Engage her in the ministry by encouraging her to record and edit a video to promote the next youth mission trip and post this across YouTube and Facebook. Equip Savannah with a script, parameters and permission to create a film that will promote a social cause to her own peers.

Lead your teens toward discipleship and service without pushing them into burnout.

There is a real danger lurking on the outskirts of your passion to see these teens engage the church and grow in the Christian life. That danger is overzealousness. Believe it or not, your teens have a life outside of the church. Like a tightrope walker, you have to maintain a balancing act that leads your teens toward discipleship and service without burning them out like a candle burning at both ends.

This is another reason to have parents involved in your youth ministry. The regular presence of parents will help remind you and fellow youth workers that these teens have families and schedules outside of your ministry events.

Encourage and equip varying personalities in your student ministry.

All men might be created *equal*, but all teens are not created *alike*. And that's a good thing, but it does present some challenges. For every varied personality in your youth group, you'll need a unique way to engage that kid and challenge him or her to grow their fullest potential in Christ.

Prepare to respond to a wide range of personalities in your student ministry. Some kids are extroverts and some introverts. Some want to visit the elderly and mow old Mrs. Evelyn's lawn. Others prefer to sit at the local Starbucks and debate the hidden Christological meanings they found in the latest Hollywood blockbuster.

It's your responsibility to meet each of these teens at their own levels, and to grow them into deeper levels of worship, discipleship and service.

Object Lesson:
Every Youth Group Has A Jason.

Let me tell you about Jason. Jason was a kid who grew up in the church where I served as Middle School Pastor.

Every Wednesday night at our youth worship service, Jason was a handful. He was a good kid, but he just couldn't seem to keep himself out of trouble during service. He would drag into the youth room after the rest of the teens had already come in, then talk to whoever was next to him all during worship.

He was a distraction - to put it charitably.

For as much as he appeared to like our church,

he loathed the teen worship service. It wasn't until one of our youth worker volunteers really started asking Jason some questions that we discovered why.

Jason just didn't appreciate expressing himself through music and lyrics. He didn't enjoy the worship services like the rest of the teens.

"Frankly," he told us, "I'd rather be swinging a hammer or painting a fence for somebody."

Jason was a *doer*, and *doing* isn't something that really fit into our definition of contemporary worship that is so often wrapped up in music or song. So, a kid like Jason is made to feel *unspiritual,* or even unwelcome, if there are no opportunities offered for worship in other forms.

Because of Jason, our leadership developed a broader scope of worship/service opportunities for the teens. From then on, Jason and other teens were given plenty of opportunities to roll up their sleeves and worship God through sweat and service.

If not for this realization, Jason (and other teens) could have simply muddled through his years in the youth group as a frustrated lump of unrealized teenage potential. Now, I can happily report that Jason is one of the most dedicated teens to ever come through that youth group.

Does your youth group have a Jason in it? Or a Savannah? I'm going to go out on a limb and say, probably.

When you really look deeper into who your teens are/what they are passionate about, you'll find ways to draw out some amazing gifts, talents and desires. Use those things, those interests and passions, to pave a path to discipleship.

Savvy Savannah doesn't need to make videos to simply impress her friends. She *needs* to be led to deeper discipleship.

Jason doesn't need to swing a hammer just because he would rather be outside in the sun. He *needs* to be led to deeper discipleship.

As a youth worker, you can not change the hearts of your teens. You can't force them to do more or give more for the sake of Christ. But, you can create an environment that empowers teens to realize where their passions and discipleship in Christ meet.

Don't be afraid to expect more from teens.

LIE #4
GREAT YOUTH PASTORS GO SOLO

Lone Rangers don't do well in ministry. They tend to find themselves...well, lonely. Get this in your head now. No matter how charismatic your personality or how incredibly skilled you are at your job; you are not meant to go it alone when ministering to God's people.

Period.

The church is the body of Christ, and body of Christ is made up of many parts that must work together if the body is going to work at all. Remember, when Christ sent his disciples out to minister to people, He sent them in groups of two or more.

There's a reason for that. Lone wolf Christians just don't make it very far. There are simply too many dangers, trials, tribulations and temptations.

To do ministry properly requires teamwork. You need trusted allies to cover your weaknesses and share the burden. That doesn't mean abdicating your role in leadership. A team needs a leader, which is what you have been called to be.

Leadership is all about communication.

Communication is all about vision. Vision is all about details. Your job as the leader is to communicate the harsh realities and disappointments, as well as the blessings and "atta-boys!"

Object Lesson:
The Jelly:Peanut Butter Ratio

One Saturday afternoon my wife, Elaina, made us both some sandwiches for lunch while I finished up some household chores. She made my favorite guilty pleasure - peanut butter and jelly.

A few bites into my sandwich, I realized something was wrong; something was very, very wrong.

Elaina made my sandwich heavy on the jelly and light on the peanut butter, when everyone knows a properly made PB&J is heavy on the PB and light on the J.

I tend to prefer much more peanut butter on my sandwich than what is probably considered normal. At the same time, I'm much more reserved in my application of jellies and jams than the average American male.

But sometimes discretion is the better part of valor. Looking first at my partially consumed PB&J, then looking into the smiling face of my lovely bride, I realized I had a proverbial bridge to cross - one that was best treaded upon delicately.

"Elaina, my oh-so-dear and lovely wife whom I cherish," I said. "I have only now realized that I may have a particular preference for how a PB&J sandwich is prepared," I said. "If ever in the future you should ever dain to prepare for me another peanut butter and jelly sandwich, could you, perhaps, go light on the jelly and heavy on the peanut butter?"

I'm sure Elaina thought my request was endearing, if a touch weird. She just reached out and touched my hand with a look on her face that seemed to say, *Bless his little heart.*

He who has ears to hear, let him hear!

In that moment early in our marriage, I discovered what appeared to be an innocuous request, really demonstrated a lesson in communicating expectations. Just because two people love each other and get married doesn't mean they like their PB&J sandwiches made the same way.

Selah.

Just because you go to the same church with somebody, or share a passion for youth ministry with other people, doesn't mean you see eye-to-eye on everything. Communication of expectations is key.

Your team's effectiveness depends on your ability to communicate the *what, where, when, why* and *who* of every situation. When preparing to communicate goals to your team, or to execute an event where you need to delegate responsibility to others, remember the Jelly:Peanut Butter Ratio. If you are to succeed in multiplying yourself, delegating responsibility and leading your youth ministry you must become a master of communicating expectations.

In the absence of communication, the worst will be assumed, I've heard my father-in-law say more times than I can count. My wife has repeated it to me several times as well.

The principle behind that sage bit of advice is simple: If you, the leader, do not communicate expectations and responsibilities in a consistent manner to your team, then assumptions and rumors will fill the void.

Don't believe it? Test it for yourself.

Go on. I dare you.

I know. I experienced such a failure.

At a church where I acted as Student Minister, I failed to communicate expectations to the volunteers who led the Sunday morning Bible study for the Middle School class. It caused some hurt feelings and one of them nearly quit out right.

Fortunately, they cared enough about the teens, the ministry and me to confront me with the situation. They told me they felt unimportant. According to them, I had gradually begun taking over more and more of their teaching duties, and pulling responsibility and involvement away from them.

They were right.

Though it was not my intention, I was boxing them out of ministry responsibilities because I felt it was easier to do it myself than train somebody else to do it. I had assumed they would naturally appreciate a lighter load with less commitment to teaching each week.

I failed to inform them of what new curriculum we would use in the coming months. I simply sprung the change on them the day of, which gave me more justification for taking the teaching duties upon myself.

In my mind, I was saving them the trouble them with having to learn the new material. In reality, they were simply sitting in class *not* teaching, while I was hogging control of everything.

Most of us can look back on the arguments, outbursts and heated debates in our lives and attribute the majority of them to simple miscommunication. At some point in the process, regardless of whether your relationship was business, personal, ministry, marriage or friendship, the person with the information did not properly distribute that information and confusion ensued.

The bottom line: If you were responsible for getting the word out, but you didn't tell the other person what they needed to know, *or* neglected to confirm that they *understood* what you were trying to communicate, you failed.

> *In the Absence of Communication, the Worst Will be Assumed.*
> *- Edwin McKnight*

Ouch. *Harsh!*

Loaded assumptions + lack of communication = fatal diagnosis for your team

My lack of communication led my volunteers to believe they were unimportant. The felt they were being pushed out of their Bible teaching responsibilities for reasons unknown to them. They assumed I didn't respect them, or that I believed they were incapable of teaching our teens.

When they finally confronted me about it, I'll be honest, their words stung. A lot. But, they were right. It was my responsibility to take ownership of my problem and correct it.

As a youth minister, you are a leader. You must communicate, set expectations and goals, be clear, be open, ask for feedback repeatedly and take ownership of the situation.

A useful bit of wisdom to remember: When a team has a problem, most often, it can be directly linked to the leadership.

Forrest Mars, Jr., heir to the Mars, Inc fortune (the company that makes M&Ms and Snickers candy bars) once said, "When you measure your own progress by the growth of those around you, we are all certain to prosper."

The first time I read this quote I honestly rejected its simple wisdom. I couldn't see how helping others to succeed did anything but take my focus away from my job. But, somehow this quote stuck in my head, like the catchy jingle for the food chopper you saw on late-night TV.

In youth ministry, you can't fly solo. Success must be mutual. When you lead your team to succeed, then *you* succeed indeed.

Oh, that rhymed.

The quote implies that we should take responsibility for the success of others in our sphere of influence. That is how we should measure our own progress.

As youth workers and student pastors, how do we define ministry success? Attendance numbers are easily measurable, but does that number quantify real discipleship? A winter retreat to the ski slopes without an injury is always a good thing, but is that all you can point to as a marker of success; no broken bones and high attendance numbers? Just another day in youth ministry, right?

What if we tried looking at the people around us for the signs of success? Forget taking an approval poll on your sermon style. And, leave the attendance record out of the equation for awhile. Look to the people in your sphere of influence: your volunteers, the families and the church staff.

Three Groups that Measure Your Success

Volunteers: Your closest companions in ministry should be growing in love for the ministry. Are you doing your part to influence and support their success in ministry? Are you watching for signs of burnout? Are you actively developing your volunteers?

Families of Your Teens: Are the hearts of the children being turned back toward their parents? Are the parents empowered to lead the spiritual and emotional education of their teenagers? Are you cheering the parents on and listening to their hearts?

Church Staff: Are fellow pastors trusting you with more of the duties they once felt only they could handle? Are you supporting the efforts of other ministries besides your own? Are your efforts in sync with the vision and mission of the senior staff? Do the other staff and pastors clearly understand your goals for ministry and know they can trust you?

Redirect your measure of success with an outward focus on the progress of others in your sphere of influence rather than yourself. After all, *whoever wants to become great among you must be your servant.* - Mark 10:43

But, don't forget that while you are pouring yourself into a team of fellow youth workers, you need someone to pour into your life as well. Yes, you need a team beside you, but you also need a mentor to guide you.

> *When you measure your own progress by the growth of those around you, we are all certain to prosper.*
> *- Forrest E. Mars Jr.*

Utilize the wisdom of those who have *been there/done that*

A wise youth worker draws on the wisdom of those who *have been there/done.* If you're not being coached by an elder, pastor or fellow youth pastor, you're missing out.

In the professional world, supervisors and managers are hired to not only to make sure you are staying on task, but to coach you in doing your job the best way possible. Your church might not present such a business model to their staff, and that's a pity.

Don't be hesitant to reach out to the other pastors, staff members or even other more seasoned youth pastors for some coaching. I can't stress enough how important it is to your ministry, your team and to your own spiritual health for you to have a mentor in the ministry.

Don't be too shy or too proud to seek one out. Approach your pastor, a trusted elder or simply a more mature youth pastor about starting a mentor relationship with you.

There is a more convenient, though I'd argue a less fulfilling, option to a personal mentorship. If there is no one you can turn to at your church or circle of ministry friend, you can find help online.

At the end of this chapter I've listed some of my favorite youth ministry blogs and websites where you can learn from other youth pastors who have already *been there/done that*. Check them out when you have a free minute.

We all need over-site from a trusted mentor not only to assure that we are doing our jobs as youth workers to the best of our abilities, but to also guard our spiritual health. I'll cover more on this subject in Chapter 8. For now, just remember that being part of the body of Christ means that someone in that body needs to lead you, in the same way that you lead your team of fellow youth workers.

A healthy youth worker needs to function in a team and be coached by a mentor. Healthy youth workers thrive. Lone rangers don't.

Online resources:

http://youthministry360.com
http://www.rethinkingyouthministry.com
http://www.simplyyouthministry.com

LIE #5
TEENS HATE LEARNING ABOUT THE BIBLE

Let's be honest. Teenagers, as an audience, have far too many things competing for their attention. With pop-culture media constantly at their fingertips, today's generation of preteens and teens are wired for distraction. Trying to introduce disciplines like daily prayer, devotional time and regular Bible reading can feel like a lost cause. You probably already notice one or two middle schoolers in the peanut gallery texting through your sermon.

What can you do?

Lose your cool? Start calling them every name in the book? Violently smashing anything within a 10 foot radius?

Probably not. Not only is that *not* what Jesus would do, it will get you fired.

> *If your plan is for a year, plant rice. If your plan is for a decade, plant trees. If our plan is for a lifetime, educate children.*
> — Confucius

The truth is, for the most part your students want to learn. And, yes, they want to learn about the Bible. They just might not know it yet.

Now, let me preempt what I'm about to say by stating that students must share a responsibility for their learning/discipling experience. The teens must be at least marginally involved in the teaching/learning atmosphere.

If a teen simply doesn't want to be there, if she is dragged to church by their parents and loathes every minute spent in your sight, you've got a bigger problem than someone texting during your Sunday School class. That situation requires engaging both the student and her family on a more personal level.

Let me say it again - teens want to learn about the Bible...they just don't know it yet. Your job is to engage them. This age group is naturally curious about, well, just about everything. That natural curiosity can lend itself to thick discussions about eternity, moral absolutes, sexuality, evidence of miracles and even questions like, "When my dog dies, will he go to Heaven?"

As you've probably already experienced, teenagers also have a pervasive sense of snarky skepticism. Which means you'll hear things like, "Seriously? Does the Bible *reeeeally* say that?"

Which gives you the perfect opportunity to say. something like, "You tell me. Let's look it up together and find out what the Bible *reeeeally* says."

If you need more proof that teens desire to dig deeper into their faith and want to learn more about the Bible, check out what the Barna Group has to say. Here are a few of the top reasons the research company found that young people say they are leaving the church as soon as they get the chance:[7]

"the Bible is not taught clearly or often enough" (23%)

...They do not feel safe admitting that sometimes Christianity does not make sense. In addition, many feel that the church's response to doubt is trivial. Some of the perceptions in this regard include not being able "to ask my most pressing life questions in church" (36%)

Do you see? Honest engagement with teens regarding the Scriptures is ripe for genuine discussion, reflective soul searching and maybe even a little biblical education. Teens don't want shallow church. As a youth minister, your job is to provide an environment that is conducive to discussion and biblical education.

But youth ministry is unlike any other ministry in the church. Your senior pastor must successfully supply quality biblical education to an adult audience; otherwise they'll stop coming. The children's pastor must engage children with biblical education on an age appropriate level; or the parents will take their kids to another church.

---

[7] The BARNA Group's findings on why teens are leaving the church:
http://www.barna.org/teens-next-gen-articles/528-six-reasons-young-christians-leave-church

But a youth pastor can spoon feed mediocre biblical teaching, and as long as the teens are entertained they'll keep coming back for more pabulum. The parents are typically just happy to know their teens are in church, so they probably won't complain either.

This is a dangerous situation.

It isn't until these teens grow up and leave the youth group that they find you failed them. Failed to teach them. Failed to disciple them. Failed to prepare them to engage a world that does not believe in their God, or any other god for that matter.

The Barna Group study previously cited gives credence to the desperate need for strong biblical teaching that engages teens. Not only is it desperately needed, but according to the Barna Group, teens desperately want it.

Great. So, kids need and want to know the Bible. What exactly are you supposed to do now? Well, it's all in the preparation and execution.

Preparation:

Proper prior planning prevents poor performance. Think like a Boy Scout and *Be Prepared*. It is your responsibility and no one can do it for you.

You must prepare. Don't wing it. You can't teach the Bible *off the cuff*. This is not your 4th grade presentation on your pet hamster. This is God's Holy Word. Treat it that way.

If you're intent on making ministry your vocation, let me strongly recommend seminary or university level courses in biblical theology. If getting a degree isn't your cup of tea, you should still audit some Bible courses. It will expose you to different ways of thinking about the Scriptures and open your mind to some amazing truths from the Scriptures you just can't pick up anywhere else.

If you're a volunteer youth worker, I still recommend auditing a university level course in biblical theology. If you don't have access to a local college or university, check out online resources, or ask your pastor for any good commentaries or other books that you might borrow.

Check out the end of this chapter for a list of books I highly recommend.

Execution:

You've prepared. Now it's time to communicate. Remember these three things when it's time to teach:

1) Create a Secure Environment

Ask yourself if the room you're teaching in is too hot or too cold? Are there enough chairs for the expected number of teens and visitors? Do you even want to use chairs? Couches? Make 'em stand the whole time?

When you introduce the lesson, create a culture of security. Let your students know they are allowed to ask questions (related to the lesson, of course). Something I regularly announce to my students is, "Any of you are allowed to stop the lesson and interrupt me with any question you may have about the Bible. Just keep your questions focused on the Bible. Don't ask me, *what's my favorite movie?* or *when did I start losing my hair?"* This lets them hear your sincerity and sets them at ease. And, let them know that there are no dumb questions. Never assume that because a teen has attended church since they were a child, they actually understand any of the fundamentals of the Christian faith.

> *In teaching you cannot see the fruit of a day's work. It is invisible and remains so, maybe for twenty years.*
> *- Jacques Barzun*

2) Come Loaded for Bear

Be ready to answer the tough questions with biblical backing. If you open up to your teens and allow them to ask questions in a culture of security where they can really explore their faith, you better be ready for more than just *where do babies come from?*

Get ready to address controversial issues like homosexuality, bisexuality, suicide, evolution, the after-life, and to answer - or at least acknowledge - you don't know the answer to questions like *why did God allow Satan to tempt Job?* Or, *why do bad things happen to good people?*

Trust me - this is not a place where you want to go it alone. Make sure any answers you provide are in keeping with the Scriptures, and it doesn't hurt if you speak with one voice with the pastoral staff at your church.

Encourage your teens to seek the counsel of their parents. This is your ultimate goal and most important calling: to turn the hearts of the children toward their parents, and the heart of the parents toward their children.

Parents should be their children's first ministers. Empower them to do so and direct the students to go to their parents for guidance and learning.

Above all, make sure you communicate with the parents regarding what you are teaching their children and how you are teaching it.

If you decide your students need to hear from you on cultural hot topics such as sexuality, you need to inform the parents first. Remember, you're dealing with young impressionable minds and Holy Scripture, which can be a volatile combination if you don't teach with respect.

Parents want to know what you're teaching their kids, especially if there's a chance it's going to cause their child to bring up awkward questions at home. They want to be prepared. Share your teaching plans with your parents. Seek out their thoughts and opinions and let them voice their concerns. The last thing you want is for one of your students to blindside their parents with an off-the-wall rant and attribute it to you.

By giving the parents a say and a platform within your teaching ministry, you empower them to better minister to their children in their own homes.

Ultimately, that's what you are hoping for. Right?

Recommended Reading

101 Things Everyone Should Know About the Bible; Rev. John Trigilo Jr., Ph.D., Th.d. and Rev. Kenneth Brighenti, Ph.D.; Adams Media, 2006

Who's Who and Where's Where in the Bible; Stephen M. Miller, Barbour Books, 2004

The Complete Bible Answer Book, Hank Hannegraaff, Thomas Nelson, 2009

LIE #6
LOSING COOL POINTS WITH TEENS IS FATAL

Most youth pastors secretly dream of impressing teens with both their ninja-like ping pong skills and their super-righteous discipleship skills. I mean, who wouldn't love a mentor who can quote the entire book of Revelation while deftly guiding a group of teens on a category 4 white water rafting trip?

Sounds amazing, right? I mean, who wouldn't want to be that kind of youth pastor?

But, beware the danger of coveting *cool points* with your teens. There's a significant difference between desiring the respect of your teens and focusing all your energy on staying cool with them.

I use the terms *staying cool/being cool/cool points* as a means of labeling the dangerous and often harmful aim of well-meaning youth workers - just like you and me. That's because confusion enters in when we as youth workers don't define and maintain the boundary that separates student from teacher and teen from youth worker.

It's similar to a parent who tells their child, "I'm not here to be your friend. I'm your parent."

You may not have been raised with this kind of

relationship with your parents, but I think you can understand what I am talking about. It can be very difficult to deliver admonishment to a student, when your aim to impress and *stay cool* with them is clouding your judgment. A parent's priority is not to impress their child but to protect, provide for, and teach them. Your calling as a youth worker includes a similar job description.

Part of our job is to provide a safe environment that facilitates events where biblical teaching and God-honoring friendships can flourish. But, to maintain that environment for the sake of one of the students - or for the sake of the whole group - might require you to say, *No!* even when the teens clamor for you to say, *Yes!*

I want to be sure you don't misunderstand me: When I tell you to establish a boundary of separation with your teens, I'm not saying that a friendship should not exist between you and your students. In fact, a healthy friendship with a respected mentor is beneficial for many teens.

The separation I am talking about involves the difference between being a friend versus being a peer.

Friendship may exist between people of different backgrounds and with a difference of decades in their respective ages. But, being a *peer* means going through the same life experience at the same time.

You are not a peer to your students; and, they are not your peers.

Consider your age, your lifestyle, your education,

your maturity, your spiritual progression, your career choice and your work experience. All of these elements of your life should be significantly advanced beyond that of your students.

I'm not saying you have to be least 20 years older than the oldest teen in the youth group, or that you must be able to recite the first five books of the Bible from memory. But there should be a difference in maturity and life story; one that is significant and apparent enough that you could easily say, "The teens and I, we are *not* peers."

Here's a situation I experienced when this boundary was not respected.

I attended an inner city church in Nashville for a short time, where the attendance numbers had dwindled over the previous years. When it came to recruiting volunteers to serve in various ministries, the pool of capable and available leaders was slim. For the most part, the mantle of leader was unceremoniously bestowed upon whoever had been voluntarily active in a particular ministry the longest.

I'd begun attending the youth group at this church as a 22 year-old investigating my calling to vocational ministry.

The lead youth pastor, Jake, was a year younger than I. He'd grown up in this church since he was a child. He was also an elder at the church and part-time janitor while attending university full-time. Jake had been dating one of the girls in the youth group for a little over a year. Though she was still in high school, she was 18 years old at the time, so there was no legal issue. But there was a huge relational issue when Jake and his girlfriend went through a very nasty break-up.

The older teens in the youth group were divided between taking sides with him or her. Several events were ill-attended due to the animosity felt among the teens. It nearly destroyed the ministry.

You see, Jake crossed a line and didn't keep the boundaries of a mentor/teacher/youth pastor. And, it cost all of us.

Maintaining appropriate boundaries can't be stressed enough, but I also must stress that staying informed and up-to-date on pop-youth-culture is extremely important as well. Do not use respecting boundaries as an excuse to remain ignorant about current trends in youth culture.

As youth workers, we have a responsibility to know the world our teens inhabit. You need to know the music, movies and idols (irony) that are hot in the eyes of your teens. Remember, they live a life outside of the walls of your youth group, and that world is full of messages influencing them to move in a thousand different directions.

Do you have a plan to combat those messages?

Allow me to suggest a good way to stay informed with teen culture and popular trends without being sucked into their world. A good offense is the best defense. That is to say, if you learn about teen culture so well that you can quote their own celebrities in a sermon, you can use it to prove the lost and fallen nature of this world while lifting up Christ and His kingdom.

Don't be afraid to mention which celebrity recently was arrested for Driving Under the Influence to communicate that consequences come with your actions.

It's okay to ask your teens how they feel about the latest recording artist who set their hotel room on fire *just because they can.*

Talk to them about why a famous celebrity millionaire might want to shoplift a scarf when she could afford to buy the store.

Know the teen culture. Use it to your own advantage. Take the daily celebrity gossip the kids are already talking about at school and transform it into a lesson in choices, money, forgiveness and judgment.

Surf Internet sites like Yahoo! and Twitter to see what stories are trending and discover what your students might already be talking about.

Don't be afraid of the blacklash that can come from calling a teen out. Sometimes, while keeping those relational boundaries between your students, you'll be forced to tell a teen *No* or you might even have to resort to the dreaded, B*ecause I said so.*

Approach these moments when you have to administer discipline as a learning experience, not only for them but for you too. It's never fun, but if handled properly, it can cause your teens to grow to respect you and trust your decisions.

Even in the most confrontational moments when you know your next words are going to cause you to lose some serious cool points, there is a wonderful opportunity for emotional and spiritual growth in your students.

I can remember a particular high school student who could be a bit of a bully in our youth group. During a weekend event with the teens, he barked at most of the other teens and bossed them around until I'd had enough.

He'd already been called out by several adult volunteers and begrudgingly complied. I personally warned him that his rude behavior was not welcome at our youth group event. During a particular small group discipleship study he went too far by loudly making fun of one of the other students who asked what he thought was a stupid question.

I immediately shut down his comments and informed him that he'd disrespected me and every one of the other students with his behavior. But, the look in his eyes told me my words had not yet affected him.

I took it a step further. I told him that he was no longer allowed to talk the rest of the night. He looked at me in disbelief.

"You really expect me to not talk all night?"

I shut him up by saying firmly, "Don't talk. You're not allowed to say anything."

This got his attention. His mouth closed and his eyes widened. I went on to say, "You will not talk. You will not ask any questions during the Bible study. If you have some earth-shattering question about God, Jesus, Heaven or Hell; you cannot ask it. I don't care how important the question is. You cannot talk."

This meant something to him.

I'd established with the teens in this particular youth ministry that they could interrupt me during Bible study at any time to ask me any question relating to the Bible. I'd built a culture of trust and honesty with these teens. They knew they could ask me anything and I would be real with them.

But, I just took that away from this kid.

He put his hands over his face and silently started to cry. This was a 17-year-old kid who moments earlier was bullying his own peers. I'd certainly lost cool points with him.

Later that evening, I apologized for hurting his feelings, but I told him I would do it all over again. He began to grow up that day. He was a very different person after that night.

Learn to see the value in keeping the appropriate boundaries between you and the teens. Don't be afraid to confront them, in love, regarding their behavior or disobedience.

You may lose cool points. But, you'll earn their respect.

LIE #7
YOUR PERSONAL SPIRITUAL HEALTH CAN WAIT

Take a quick inventory.

Do you feel like you live out of the church's office more than your house?

Can you remember the last time you studied the Bible outside of preparing for a sermon?

How many nights a week do you spend in ministry events away from your family?

Does your idea of getting closer to God only involve dedicating more time and energy to the youth ministry?

If you cringed when you answered any of the above questions, your spiritual health is in need of a serious check-up.

Maintaining your spiritual health isn't just about keeping your prayer life alive. It also includes your physical and mental well being. As a youth worker, you need to pay special care to your whole self - body, mind, and soul.

If you've been a youth worker for any length of time at all, you already know what a drain this ministry can be on your physical body. (If you're new to youth ministry, just give it time; you'll understand what I mean.) Between planning and attending youth services, participating in pick-up games of basketball/football/soccer/ping-pong, showing up at the occasional high school football game/ wrestling match/ swim meet/ choir performance/ theater production, spending a week at summer camp, staying up all night at the lock-in and chaperoning the weekend middle school retreat you can expect to average about 4 good nights of sleep...per month.

Rest, re-creation and rejuvenation is necessary. And it's Biblical, too!

Finding time to pause, rest, and rejuvenate is not only necessary, it's also biblical. Think about how many times Jesus withdrew into the desert, away from the crowds He was called to minister to. Sometimes He went alone. Other times He took his closest friends, His disciples, along with Him.

When you get right down to it, God Himself rested after creating the universe...and He said it was Good!

He even thought dedicating a portion of the week to rest and to honor Him was pretty important. That particular commandment even made the Big Ten; that's how important God thinks rest is.

Your work in ministry shouldn't be a crutch, allowing you to be so busy that you can disobey His command. Seriously, you can't expect to be successful leading the next generation *toward* Christ if you allow your ministry schedule to lead you *away* from Christ.

On a purely practical level, rest and rejuvenation is just good sense. Let's see how many quaint examples I can come up with:

The lumberjack needs to sharpen his ax.
The cook needs to cleanse her pallet.
The race car driver needs a pit stop.
Every army needs to eat.
A bear needs to hibernate.
The youth worker needs a dedicated time of rest.

Okay, so that last one isn't a quaint example, but you get the point.

My friend Jasper Rains from Get Real Youth Ministries admits to experiencing occasional burn-out.

"I have been known to overwork a bit," Jasper confesses. "I burn the candles at both ends (and sometimes in the middle) a lot. This can run into some serious issues for my spirituality. When I am run down, my guard falls and sin becomes easier to justify. My angry inner man comes out. I get lethargic. My days in professional Christianity lead me to professional hypocrisy from time to time."

You are no different. Being called by God to this ministry does not mean you are superhuman. You were not endowed with a special blanket of spiritual essence that magically deflects weariness, frustration, burn-out and fatigue. God's grace is sufficient, but you have an obligation to operate within the blessing of that grace responsibly, not recklessly.

Get rested. Get fed. *Then* get going.

But it's not just your bodily health that you have to be concerned with. Your mind and heart get a non-stop workout, too. The burden of youth ministry can be a heavy one, as you listen to hurtful stories of broken families. Teens will confess their innermost fears and secret vices to you. Parents will question your motives and tactics. Sometimes you play the role of confidant, sometimes you play referee and sometimes you have to be a disciplinarian.

It's enough to wear anyone down.

Jasper offers some great points for how to find both physical and spiritual rest below. For more suggestions, visit his blog at:
http://youthministerman.blogspot.com

1. Vacation Away - I don't think there is anything better than getting away from it all. *Stay-cations* seldom work for those in ministry. If you stay, people will find you. Vacationing away from home and spending time with your family or friends is crucial to recharging.

2. Unplug - Maybe you don't have the luxury of a get-away vacation, but you can still recharge your batteries by unplugging from things that drain you. Technology is a wonderful thing, but there is such a thing as being too connected.

    Take a media fast.
    Turn the cell phone off.
    Leave the laptop at the office.

Simply step away.

This can be for one night or a week of evenings. The voice mails, emails, tweets and Facebook messages will still be there when you plug back in. Trust me - the world will continue without being in constant contact with you.

3. Step Away During The Day - Take a few minutes during the day and leave your office. If it is a nice day, take a walk. If weather is bad, drive to the library, or a museum or a store you enjoy and spend half an hour window shopping. Taking a few minutes away from the workaday world can be key to surviving those inevitable times of stress.

4. Stop For Time With God - This is a definite need everyday. After all, you *are* in ministry, right? Staying charged by reading God's Word and praying is an essential part of your preparation - not only for the week's events, but for your own spiritual health.

Don't rush through this time. Take it slow and make it meaningful. Feel free to sing a song of worship after reading and praying. You can't stay charged if you are not plugging into the ultimate source of rest.

Jasper's words about spending time with God reminds me of another important concept - practicing Sabbath. The Sabbath is a biblical mandate for a period of rest within a week's time.

Notice, I said it's a mandate...not a suggestion.

Christians might vigorously debate whether the Sabbath falls on a Saturday or a Sunday. Don't let yourself get bogged down in the technical details of *when* the Sabbath should take place. Rather, concentrate on *what* the Sabbath is!

Consider what the Bible has to say about the Sabbath:

Exodus 20:11 - *Therefore the LORD blessed the Sabbath day and made it holy.*
Exodus 20:8 - *Remember the Sabbath day by keeping it holy.*
Exodus 20:10 - *On [the Sabbath] you shall not do any work.*

First note that God himself created the Sabbath and declared it holy. Next, He instructed that we, his children, should honor and remember the Sabbath day. Last, one of the most essential means of honoring the Sabbath day is to stay away from work.

Do you need to read that again, Dear Youth Worker?

No work on the Sabbath.

This means you! Put the phone down and turn the computer off. And, lest you think the Sabbath is only all about sleeping in, remember - you are commanded to honor it and keep it holy.

How?

How about cracking open the Bible for more than 10 minutes? Maybe study God's word for more than just the purpose of writing your next sermon.

Try spending time in prayer in during the Sabbath. Take the opportunity to clear out all the noise and listen, truly listen, to God's voice.

Your spiritual health needs a Sabbath. You were designed for it the same way a car needs regular tune ups and maintenance. Honor the Sabbath day and keep it holy. Your health, both spiritually and physically, depends on it.

Consideration the importance of mentorship to your spiritual health.

In chapter 4 you read about the necessity of working with a strong team. It not only strengthens the youth ministry, but a strong team will also draw on mentors who oversee your personal growth and spiritual health.

But just who is a mentor? A mentor should be a trusted member of the ministry who has walked with God longer than you. This person could be a senior pastor or an elder in the church. They might be a fellow youth worker who is older and has more experience under his or her belt.

The goal in mentorship is to form a bond with the other person where coaching and teaching comes through watching, listening to and experiencing what the other person does in their day-to-day decisions within ministry.

Find a mentor. Shadow that person as they walk, teach, lead and serve. Ask questions. Ask lots of questions. It's important. You'll need the guidance of an experienced and mature spiritual leader as you walk through your own journey in ministry.

A mentor will be there to share stories with you. A mentor will listen to your frustrations. A mentor will help pick up the pieces when you experience failure and everything falls apart.

Your spiritual health is such an important thing, but it can also be a touchy and sensitive subject.

The church administrator might step in and tell you when she spots an error in your budget proposal for summer camp. Parents might alert you to safety concerns they might notice at the lock-in you're hosting. But, people are hesitant about speaking up when they notice that you're approaching spiritual burn out.

Folks tend to treat it as if it's none of their business. You can slowly spiral down into spiritual oblivion without a single person butting in.

The problem is, it's just so easy to neglect your own spiritual health for the sake of your *"ministry."* You might not even realize it yourself. You might think you just need to knuckle down work even harder.

Don't do it. You can't give out of an empty basket.

Don't neglect your spiritual health any more than you would neglect your physical health. Make it a priority.

The bottom line is, if you are not spiritually

healthy, your youth ministry won't be spiritually healthy. You won't be able to serve the sick, the needy or the hungry for very long.

LIE #8
BIGGER, FASTER AND LOUDER = BETTER

The tone, tempo and programming behind your youth ministry is important. Don't let anyone tell you different. Decisions about the quality and types of ministries available to your teens should occupy a significant portion of your time as a youth worker.

But keep in mind that bigger, faster and louder is only one facet of that programming, and it isn't even the most important thing. While you're chasing after the most exciting variation of dodge ball, or planning the next amazing retreat, don't sacrifice the spiritual welfare of your youth ministry for the *Ahhh* factor.

Check out this story from Jeremy Zach, a veteran youth pastor who works for XP3 Students.

"It was Wednesday afternoon around 3 PM, and I was in *program mode*. I was polishing my talk, running through the program schedule, reviewing the PowerPoint slides for worship, returning emails to parents and brainstorming game ideas. I was getting things done before youth group.

"Then, I had three high school students make an unexpected visit to my office.

"It was *not* during youth ministry office hours. I was immediately annoyed because I knew these students. They were talkers and I knew they really wanted my full attention...which I was not willing to give at the time.

"I spun around in my office chair and said, 'What's up?'

"One student started talking about his school day. I pretended to listen, but my mind was not focused on what he was saying. I was listening, but not *really* listening. I was to busy trying to brainstorm another great game for that night's youth group meeting.

"Eight minutes passed (not that I was not counting) and I had this random thought: *I wonder what these students really need from their youth pastor?*

"I let the student finish his story, and then I intensely looked at all three students and asked: 'In your opinion, what should be the most important task in a youth pastor's job description?'

"Without blinking an eye each one answered: 'Simply pray for us. In fact, that's why we're here. We need prayer.'

"I about had a heart attack. I had blown it. I sensed a deep conviction in my spirit. I was their youth pastor, yet I was more focused on thinking about toilet paper dodge ball than attending to their spiritual needs.

"The first thing every youth pastor should do for the students in his youth ministry is pray for them...regularly. Unfortunately, it seems that to some extent, the more experienced a youth pastor becomes, the easier it can be to focus more on programming and less on people.

"Knowing how to run a youth program is a great thing and indicates that you are a seasoned youth worker who understands the insane importance of planning. You run into trouble with your *default mode* is program and ministry management, instead of praying with and for your students.

"Mark chapter 9: 28& 29 says:

"After Jesus had gone indoors, his disciples asked him privately, 'Why couldn't we drive it out?' He replied, 'This kind can come out only by prayer.'

"Even the disciples sometimes forgot to pray when they were totally focused on doing ministry. The disciples thought they were seasoned ministers. They were hanging and traveling with Jesus and they still forgot to pray.

"For my first two years in youth ministry, I used to pray in my office every Sunday morning for my students. Five years into my youth ministry career, I was only praying from the front of the stage because it was a great transitional piece to the youth group program.

"Somewhere along the line, I stopped praying for my students.

"That day in my office, those three students gave me profound and practical insight into what should be our top priority as youth leaders. I have never forgotten the lesson that I learned on that

Wednesday afternoon, four hours before youth group."8

Wow. Those are some really honest words from a seasoned youth pastor.

Jeremy just laid out for you one of the biggest traps in youth ministry. As a youth worker, you are called to be many things for the sake of the ministry. You have to wear the hat of a chauffer, a teacher, a disciplinarian, a leader, a follower...etc. Be sure not to let all the administrative aspects of your job overtake your first call - to be an intercessor and a shepherd.

Games, lights and events can add to the energy of a youth ministry, but those things aren't the core.

You've heard it before, and it might sound trite, but it's the truth: Keep the main thing the main thing.

Your essential function as a youth worker is to nurture the spiritual health of the teens. If that duty falls through the cracks in the busyness of party planning with a fog machine and programmed lights and sound, then you've failed.

I know you want things to look good and sound good. And it's okay to want those things. I want to give the best sermon presentation possible as well. But, sometimes while preparing a message, I've found myself spending more time worrying about

---

8 Check out this story and more of Jeremy's experiences at his blog, *REyouthpastor* http://www.reyouthpastor.com

whether I should use a lapel microphone or a hand-held than I do about what I'm actually teaching.

That's a shame.

Trust in power of the Gospel over the glitz of big events and loud music.

Do you really believe in the truth of the Gospel? If so, then trust in the simple power it has to change lives without the need to dress it up and sell it.

One of the biggest turn-offs that people complain about regarding the church is they feel pastors and church-folk are always trying to *sell* them this Christianity thing. It can come across as if we are trying to convince them of something that we ourselves don't quite believe ourselves.

That's not to say we shouldn't do everything with excellence in mind. We certainly should. But there is a big difference in giving the best presentation of the Gospel possible, as often as possible, and trying to sell teens on a pre-packaged faith.

As a youth worker, you know you've crossed the line when you sit down to plan your ministry year and realize your end goal is only to drum up more excitement for the next big event rather than leading teens into a deeper relationship with Jesus Christ.

Speaking of misguided goals and objectives, let me share with you some more of Jasper Rains thoughts on this topic.

"Too often it seems that our churches want to

measure success based on numbers. If we all had a dollar for the times we have asked or been asked, *how many students are in your group*, we could retire to a nice quiet condominium in a distant, foreign land.

"Numbers are important. Numerical growth is the natural outcome of spiritual growth. The problem comes when increasing attendance drives our purpose. Success in ministry does not lie with numerical changes; it lies with changes of the heart. Success is much more than having a large group. Success is developing ministers."

Well said, Jasper.

Bigger, louder and faster programming doesn't yield automatic success. Programming should be an inward focus that causes us to ask, "What does our church/ministry have to offer?"

We need to ask that question often, but the answer doesn't directly tell us what results are produced.

Pharmaceutical companies put newer drugs on the market all the time. While sales are important, the true measure of a drug's success should be measured by how well it heals the sick, rather than by how much profit the drug earns for the pharmaceutical company.

The same applies to ministry. Your measure of success does not come from the inward planning of

programs, but the outward production of disciples.
 As Jasper says, "Success is developing ministers."

LIE #9

YOUTH MINISTRY IS JUST A STEPPING STONE TO A JOB AS A REAL PASTOR

Truth be told, way too many youth pastors serving the church today are doing so because they believe youth ministry is just a way to get their foot in the door to *real* ministry.

You know those people. You might even *be* one of them.

It's understandable. It's natural to want to advance in your career. But the belief that youth ministry is just a training ground for *real* ministry, or some type of holding cell until you enter your *real* calling is nothing more than vain and misguided.

It is a self-perpetuating lie.

Just look at the collective faces of youth pastors. Most are young, under 30 years old. Most are also preparing for a future as a senior pastor.

It's not uncommon to hear comments from churchgoers and other church staff members that expose the perception of youth pastors and youth ministry as *junior varsity*. Such a perception presupposes the wider belief that your intent as a youth worker should be to graduate from the junior varsity world of youth ministry to real ministry in the big league of the adult world.

However, the truth is not so cut and dried, and it's not so...condescending.

One of the best youth pastors I know is over 40 years old.

What? You thought youth ministry was just a young person's game?

So did I, frankly.

But the reality is there are plenty of good, experienced and accomplished youth pastors who are in it for the long haul. They stick around youth ministry for decades. Believe it or not, there are youth pastors who confess to having no interest in ever becoming a senior pastor.

> *I think age is a very high price to pay for maturity.*
> *-Tom Stoppard*

Youth ministry is not just a young person's game and it certainly is not a ministry that should be relegated to a stepping stone toward some other career agenda.

In the U.S. Army, fresh, enthusiastic, but often inexperienced 2nd Lieutenants are often paired with seasoned, grizzled old platoon sergeants. The combination of leadership, experience, enthusiasm and caution results in an effective unit.

Our teens need that same kind of structure. They need passionate, enthusiastic young youth workers, but they also need mature mentors.

Every generation of teenagers have looked to young celebrities for excitement, attitude and fashion. My parents' generation had The Monkees and Bobbie Sherman. The teen idols of my generation were Zack Morris of *Saved by the Bell* and 80s boy band *New Kids on the Block*. Today's generation of teens are likely to look upon Taylor Swift and Justin Bieber as the young pop icons of the moment.

Our culture will continue to produce young celebrity idols who will gain their fifteen minutes of fame, then fade into oblivion. The teens in your ministry don't need another young idol. They have plenty to choose from. Don't waste your time trying to become the next one.

They need an adult.

They need a mature adult.

They need someone who can guide them through the path already prepared for them by disciples who have gone before us.

Your teens need a mature mentor – not an inexperienced party planner.

Consider this question: What is the true value of age in a youth pastor? Maybe try asking it this way: How many years do you think it will take for you to become a really good youth pastor?

Does that question make sense to you? Is your gut reaction something like, "I've *always* been an awesome youth pastor."

Once you've said it out loud, doesn't it sound just

a tad bit arrogant?

When I showed up at my first church assignment I just assumed I was already an amazing theologian/disciple maker. And I believed that I was the coolest Christian

> *Pride goes before destruction, a haughty spirit before a fall.*
> **– Proverbs 16:18**

any teenager was ever going to meet. Why wouldn't they want to follow in my footsteps? I believed I was well on my way to transforming any church I worked at with a movement of God that would come straight from my effortless command of the youth ministry. Before long, the kids in my youth group would be asking, "WWAD - What Would Aaron Do?"

What a load of hogwash!

I wasn't simply born an amazing youth worker. But for some reason, like so many youth workers I know, I thought that at 21 years of age I had already learned everything worth knowing; that I was destined to show all the teens and parents and pastors and *the entire church* something they have never seen before!

What arrogance.

In the professional world, you're not considered an expert at any craft, skill or trade until you have several years of experience under your belt and can demonstrate that you fully meet the requirements of certification set by industry regulators. Many corporations provide on-site training for new employees that can last from a few months to several years. Many professions require continuing education credits in order to maintain your license to work in the field.

Why is it that we, in our naivety, think that good intentions and an introductory knowledge of the Bible are sufficient to make a fully-developed youth pastor?

Just add guitar playing skills to your resume and you're a certified expert in youth ministry, right?

Let me tell you the story of Michael. Michael is grown man now. He's been a husband and father for several years. But, when Michael was only 18 years old, his church found itself in need of a new youth pastor.

It was the summer after Michael graduated from high school, and he was looking forward to future plans beyond his home town. Little did he know that he was going to be asked to stick around town a little longer.

Michael had grown up in his church, and he had graduated from high school. Apparently he cleared all the qualifications, at least as far as the senior pastor was concerned. Michael was asked to be the new youth pastor of large church in a major denomination.

At 18 years old.

It sounds ridiculous but it's true. Michael accepted the job and had a rough go of it, to put it gently.

There is a lot to be said for youth and enthusiasm, but there's something to be said for age and experience, too.

No one walks into a job thinking they know everything there is to know on Day-One. Or, even Year-One. Ministry should be the same way. Just because I started out with a lot of heart and enthusiasm years ago, doesn't mean I didn't have so much more to learn.

Honestly, older and more seasoned youth pastors tend to enjoy their jobs a lot more. Do you remember in the very first chapter, when I said my deepest worry when I started in youth ministry was that someone would think I wasn't working hard enough?

I don't worry about that anymore.

Sure, I still strive to accomplish tough goals all the time. But, I've already failed a few times... and, I've succeeded a few times too! After a few years, the worry subsides. The insecurity fades away.

My deepest concern is no longer for what other people think.

A mature and seasoned youth worker is empowered to plan and execute ministry based on sound theology, in conjunction with other church staff and pastors, and in partnership with parents. Spending years in youth ministry allows you the time to take it on the chin a few times, admit to your own mistakes and get back up to try all over again.

Make no mistake - you will stumble and you will fall sometimes. You will fail. It is inevitable. It is what you do with those failures that determine your effectiveness as a youth minister, and as a person.

What do you do with your failures? I advise you to take them directly to God and ask earnestly, "Lord, what am I supposed to learn from this?" That question, given to God, exhibits a learning attitude that is active in its response. It is a far better posture to take than a passive, and unattractive response like, "Why me?" or "How could you?"

A seasoned youth pastor is capable of handling success.

Take pivotal moments in your ministry, whether successes or failures, to God with honesty. Discover how He wants to use this failure/success/experience to further His kingdom.

Your youth ministry, as well as all other aspects of your life, will be marked by failures, but believe me, you will experience some extraordinary successes! You will see programs take off in your youth ministry. You will watch teens grow into devoted disciples and missionaries. You will train up volunteers to become the next generation of youth pastors.

How you respect that success will reveal whether you are self-less instrument in God's hands, or a loud ego with a church platform. Paul calls it being a sounding brass or a clanging cymbal.

A seasoned youth pastor is more capable of handling success. It's so easy for young man or woman to be overcome with their own initial success. Immature leaders blame the team for failure, but try to claim success for themselves alone.

A true test of maturity will be how you handle the nuances of success. Remember, from the beginning to the end, all of this came from God and is due to God for His namesake. You and I are arrows in His quiver. We are tools in the hands of a master craftsman. Give credit to the archer and due respect to the craftsman.

LIE #10
YOUTH MINISTRY IS A FAILED EXPERIMENT

Believe it or not, there are some in the church who think youth ministry is a failed experiment that is, or should be, on its way out the door.

There have been debates and heated conversations in several youth ministry circles regarding the future and legitimacy of youth ministry as we know it.

From folks who believe in the Orange strategy[9] of family ministry to the makers of the 2011 documentary called *Divided*[10], the opinions are widely varied, but all have valid points to make. In the past 10 years, youth pastors, educators and research groups have observed some of the successes of youth ministry in contrast to some of the inherit problems it faces.

My intention in ending the book with this chapter is to make you aware of some of the discussions and camps of thought that are currently

---

[9] To see what the Orange strategy is all about check out their website http://www.whatisorange.org/about-orange-strategy/
[10] See the video here - http://dividedthemovie.com/

emerging and will potentially forge the future shape of youth ministry. These discussions come from good folks who earnestly love the Church and are asking the hard questions about what has come before us in the realm of youth ministry, where we are today and what should come after us.

As with any debate, there are some who are always Debbie Downers and others who swear they can see a sunny side on the dark side of the Moon. I can only encourage you to use discernment and take any opinion with a grain of salt.

There are new models emerging for how youth ministry can create truer discipleship for teens.

I believe there are some excited thinkers out there who are currently working on a new model for how youth ministry can create truer discipleship for teens. But there are other equally passionate, and equally opinionated, voices that are clamoring for specialized ministries in the American church to be abolished.

Both of these sides of the debate are looking for change.

Pay special attention to this since you, dear youth worker, will be the one swimming in this shark-infested ocean when the tide turns. And make no mistake...the tide will turn, one way or the other.

Change is coming to youth ministry, and, I truly believe that change will be for the good of youth ministry. That is not to say that the way you and I are doing ministry right now is either right or wrong. Youth ministry, and indeed all ministry, is unique to the needs of the individual and the community. Jesus healed a number of different blind men, but he didn't heal them all the same way. He might lay His hands on one, and put mud on the eyes of another.

Your method might be different from mine, but for both of us, as in any endeavor, there is always room for improvement. The key is hearing from God and doing what we know we are called to do.

Change is coming to youth ministry.

Youth ministry is a relatively new concept in the American church. The first recognizable contemporary youth ministries didn't emerge until the last 1960s or early 1970s. We are only just now getting an accurate picture of what generations of teens look like after they have grown up through youth ministries to become adults. We are only now getting a sense of what, if any, impact youth ministry had upon their lives.

As you and I inherit the techniques and expectations of youth ministry that have developed over the past 40+ years, we should stop and make an honest assessment of what worked and what didn't' and maybe even what worked them, but doesn't work now.

Let me here unequivocally state that I do not believe that youth ministry is done.

I believe youth ministry is still in its adolescence.

It has at times, like most teenagers, been reckless and immature, stamping its feet when it didn't get its own way; stayed out past its bedtime; argued with those in authority; thought it knew what was best without seeking wise counsel and sulked with it didn't get its own way.

But I also believe youth ministry is maturing in the grand scheme of things and there are changes to come. The ongoing debate I've been talking about is about this very self-reflection into the heart of youth ministry.

As youth ministry continues to mature, I believe it is imperative that we ask those questions. We should be asking hard questions, but they should be the right questions.

For example, we should all be asking:

Does youth ministry as we are practicing it produce converts to Christ?

Does youth ministry as we are practicing it produce more dedicated disciples of Christ?

Does youth ministry as we are practicing it unite teens with their families or divide them?

Is there a better way to do specialized ministries (i.e. children's ministry, youth ministry, empty nester's Bible study) in the church than to divide families by age group and segregate them?

Has the previous generation grown more faithful to Christ due at least in part to their involvement in youth ministry?

Does youth ministry as we know it prepare teens

for the challenges that will come against their faith when they graduate into adulthood?

These are hard questions that probably can't be answered with a simple *Yes* or *No*. They are more likely to be answered with, *Sometimes*, *Maybe* or *I Don't Know*. The abstract nature of most of these questions makes it difficult to come up with any clear-cut answers.

But, if the answers to your questions, and the preponderance of statistical evidence tells us anything, it is that change is needed, [11] and it needs to come sooner rather than later.

You need to be a part of that change. You are called to this ministry; therefore, you are called to blaze the trail for its future!

Saddle up your horses. We've got a trail to blaze!

As I close out this book, I would like to offer up a few words on what I believe is needed for the future of youth ministry.

Over the course of the past few decades, several misconceptions regarding youth ministry have emerged that we must change if youth ministry is to remain a relevant and viable ministry of the church.

---

[11] I would encourage you to check out The Barna Group website – particularly, their research on youth and teens at http://www.barna.org/topics/teens-nextgen. This site should be your go-to resource for statistics on the American church.

(*If you're not sure what those misconceptions are, please read the first 9 chapters of this book.*)

The most problematic, and fortunately, the easiest to combat, is the sole reliance on a singular personality to completely carry youth ministries in our local churches. It is what some people have dubbed the *cult of personality*.

That's right. Your loveable, likeable, energetic, charismatic personality, that draws kids like flies to honey, could be the very thing that destabilizes your church's youth ministry the most. The most immediate and helpful change we do to improve youth ministry across the board is to transform the role of the youth pastor.

I don't have a catchy word for it yet.

Maybe we can call it "decentralization" or "shared responsibility" or "co-coachable discipling."

Nah, none of those really work.

Whatever you decide to call it, what I'm advocating is this: The change that youth ministries are experiencing right now, and will continue to experience in the years to come, is a need to pull away from the *cult of personality* that masquerades as leadership in youth ministry.

We must begin to move to a concept of shared responsibility of leadership and mentorship between ministry staff, parents and volunteers.

You might think, "Well, Aaron, we already have parents chaperoning our retreats and volunteers that send the email-blast to our visiting teens."

I'm not simply talking about utilizing parents as

the hands to get the busy-but-necessary work of ministry checked off your to-do list. I'm talking about actively recruiting a broad set of parents and volunteers to act as the eyes, ears and brains of the youth ministry.

Imagine it this way: A football team performs with several levels of leadership during every single play within a game. Your head coach communicates with the offensive coordinator in the booth and the defensive coach on the sidelines, while the quarterback calls out plays to the team on the field.

Each level of leadership has its own responsibilities and is able to function with a unified purpose. You never see the head coach calling the plays, then running onto the field to communicate the plays to the team, then taking the snap.

But, youth pastors are often expected to operate in that manner. At least, they might feel like they are expected to operate that way; and perception usually trumps reality.

What will such a multi-level leadership ministry look like to you?

I really don't know.

That's where the excitement is for each of us as youth workers. God is going to lead you to shape and mold your ministry to meet the needs of your community in a way that gives glory to Him.

Allow God to speak to your heart. Invite the ministry staff, parents and volunteers into a coordinated effort of prayer to discover what God's plan is for re-shaping the role of youth pastor in your church.

Wouldn't that be a wonderful thing, to have a leadership framework customized for your specific youth ministry by God himself?

Youth ministry is changing.

The future of youth ministry is changing. That makes it a little bit scary. It also makes it incredibly exciting!

God is still in control.

You still have the call to change lives by introducing Jesus Christ to the teens in your community. Let that always be your focus, and the misconceptions and outright lies about youth ministry will fade away.

THANK YOU!

The writing of this book was a journey of asking tough questions about ministry, then having to answer them. The following people deserve thanks for making this book a reality:

    Greg Creasey and Dave Mason – for asking the tough questions.
    Mike Parker – my publisher who first told me I should write this book.
    Scott Hutcheson – for finally convincing me to write the book.
    My wife, Elaina – for sharing the ups and downs of this ministry journey.
    My Mom and Dad, Valerie and Gene – you raised me and were the first to introduce this Faith to me.

www.ingramcontent.com/pod-product-compliance
Lightning Source LLC
Chambersburg PA
CBHW071409290426
44108CB00014B/1752